POEMS FOR OWEN

D1526029

POEMS FOR OWEN

Martha Gould

TORONTO
Exile Editions

1997

This edition is published by Exile Editions Limited,
20 Dale Avenue, Toronto, Ontario, Canada   M4W 1K4

Sales Distribution:
General Distribution Services
30 Lesmill Road
Don Mills, ON
M3B 2T6
1-800-387-0172

Composition and Design by MICHAEL P. CALLAGHAN
Typesetting and Layout by MOONS OF JUPITER, TORONTO
Printed and Bound by AMPERSAND PRINTING, GUELPH

The publisher wishes to acknowledge
the assistance toward publication of the Canada Council
and the Ontario Arts Council.

ISBN 1-55096-164-0

The Canada Council
Conseil des Arts du Canada

In memory of

Owen Ilkyaz Tuncali

MAY 23, 1991 – MARCH 3 + 5, 1996

18 March 1996

My Dear Owen,

I am your grandmother, your baba-anne. When I heard
the news that you were born, I could not find words to
express my happiness. You gave me the happiness of
being a grandmother, my little one.

As all the days, months, years, passed, the space
belonging to you came into being. Your photographs,
drawings and everything that came from you, every-
thing made by your little hands, are part of this space.
Every morning I start my day by saying Good Morning
to you.

You were going to come this summer. I was going to be
able to speak about your beautiful eyes, your small
hands, your feet, everything about you. I was going to
love, smell, and touch you. But since Allah loves you
more than us, Allah took you to his care, my dear
grandson. You joined Allah, my dear Owen.

Those of us left behind, those who love you, those who
know you, especially your dear mother, Martha, and
your dear father, Murat, are in incredible pain and sad-
ness, which you may not know. Perhaps it is better that
you don't know because with your sweet little heart
you could not stand our sadness and pain and who

knows what you would do to share our sadness and to console us, my little one.

It is our destiny that we have to separate without meeting each other. However, I strongly believe that we will be together in Ahret. And you will be waiting for us in the skies where you fly like an angel.

You, in this short time, perhaps came into this world to give us a lesson. To your mother, father, and to all your family you brought good luck, a good omen. You finished your duties and have gone back to Ahret.

Wish us, from wherever you are, strength and patience. Until the day we join you, we wish you all goodness and happiness and send our love to you, my little angel.

Your grandfather, your grandmother, your aunts and uncles, your cousins, all wish you comfort in your sleep my dear Owen. We are not saying goodbye to you. You are always with us. You are part of our souls, blood, tears, our whole being, my little grandson.

Mualla Tuncali

translated from Turkish by Murat Tuncali and Martha Gould

Owen   Muriet   Martha   by Owe

Contents

Where your father comes from
they make delicate glass bottles
to catch tears — grieving,
you hold them to your streaming eyes.
I fashion these gossamer words, hoping
they hold the salty water of life,
stoppered, won't let it evaporate.

Star-gazer Lilies: To Owen

I.

Oh, it's still early.
There are all these baseball noises,
and the neighbors calling their dog
who wants to get AWAY!
And I am stuck inside the house of spring,
pushing my glasses up,
unable to see out of this
opaque bubble of grief.
You are not out there,
calling your Dad
and kicking the long green leaves
of the grass, you have passed out of
all hearing and all calling;
I cannot touch you,
your beautiful growing limbs
and the small hairs on your back.
I can see where your father
measured you against the door jamb
and marked the day,

but that day has passed.
You have gone farther
than the dog wants to
or the baseball boys
have dreamed of.
I send my love after you,
the music of your name.

                    ✿   ✿   ✿

And what I think of
is how the full moon rose
over the fatal city of Toronto
like the brightest thing ever made —
but you had died, had left
your hot and shaking body
and your empty brain —
and there was the moon
reminding me how I counted
on what it promised
the day you were born,
as it rose over the wing
of the hospital, as I lay
trembling with delivering you!
Now I must relearn the moon,

its bringing and taking you,
wondering if the way it still comes up
means I am still, some here or there,
some now or then, your mother.

❀   ❀   ❀

And in the hospital
we saw the burned child
passing on a gurney,
the child's stark eyes staring
as he or she —- I do not know —
rode such a sad barge
down the cold white river.
And you were lying eyes closed
ice piled round you, you
naked among the tubes and
apparatuses,
dead once and going to die
a second time.
And that child — he or she —
may be alive,
but oh what grief the parents know,
and I know!
Losing you, having you die

is so close to the death of everything!
But not nearly as hard to bear
I think now — not knowing the outcome —
as where that burned child
travelled down the corridors
of grief and guilt
to what long end
or what new hope
I here imagine
in the stark light
of your expulsion.

❁   ❁   ❁

Everyone calls me.
I answer the telephone,
open the door as open as
an oracle, because indeed
I am suspended by a spider's web
over the chasm of grief and mystery.
Every breeze swings me,
every glimpse of a child
or young enraptured shout.
I am unable to leave my post,
so close to the jaws of death

and hearing life whispering
its lovely promises.
That you who are gone are here,
that the wild geese will go over again
like all imagined grief and keening,
that everything of the best
I found to say to you, you in
your young life, will have
these same wings
and survive on air and longing.

      ✿   ✿   ✿

This is not mourning,
this is love that has no end.
I imagine you as my friend,
bone of my bone,
home of my home —
and there is no loneliness
in love like this!
This is all giving,
and in the living is the loss,
and that we must somehow
come to accept.

As I accept
the death of the baby mouse
our cat has brought in
and played with, and let escape
into the cold air vent
that runs deep inside
the structure of our house.

      ◈   ◈   ◈

But now the children are going home,
their parents are gathering them
from the baseball fields and shepherding them
into the vans for the drive toward bath and bed,
and school tomorrow.
The yellow buses burrow
through my day like moles;
yours gears up to pass our house
where once it slowed to let you off.
Every day I am waiting at
the same time and place for life
to snap back and let you off again
in the spring, as it should,
you with your shout and welcoming.
You knew I would be there,

you did not doubt,
and oh, I would not let you.
I would be there like some fixture
the sun saw every day
as it passed on its
important business.
But now you do not come.
The yellow bus passes,
indifferent as the sun.

❂   ❂   ❂

Some one is hurrying by in a car,
and beeping, as though
they haven't heard that death is!
Surely they could slow
and let whatever live thing
there was in the road pass by,
blessed.
Surely they could recognize
the same life in the skating child,
the inching worm, the slinking cat —
and with that, hold a foot
off the gas, a hand off the horn.
Oh, we are born into something

bigger than us, and everything great
is in seeing that, and living
as though your part were as
small as the part of a gnat
but essential,
necessary.

✤   ✤   ✤

And so you only answer me
from the small confines of my heart.
You were here, and you are gone,
and whatever I am is supposed
to live with that. As the sky knows
the comet, not as the grass recognizes
the superior strength of the dandelion!

No, I do not know what to do,
or how to accept your death.
Surely it is your life that most
perplexes me. We gave you strength
and the artesian fountains of our ancestors,
and yet you departed out of this life
and are where I cannot follow or find you.
Sometimes the water runs away

down the hill, nourishing a fern
but not stopping its impatient journey.
So I begrudge the sea.
The sea that grounds you.

     ✣   ✣   ✣

You see you have left me
grappling with the stars
and with my own death.
There is nothing I could not lose
now that you are dead.
You are like the thunderbolt
coming to disarm the house
and free the electricity.
Now I cannot connect.

But more than that
I am like the absence
of the well-loved lily
in the old garden —
every year it has graced the path
and suddenly, one spring,
there is nothing!
How is a person like me

to understand that,
when everything I have known
has come up in you?

     ❂   ❂   ❂

So, I am here with the sibyls,
suspended over the caverns of death,
drunk on the breath of the hoya
and the smell of fresh bread.
So I say: play with the cat,
and listen my dears to that old refrain
of the robin, minding its young
and charming the worms out of the ground,
that sound of spring, of everything
that we know, that we both recognize
and remember as though it were the first time
and the eons between.
See what I mean?
The worm is what we know,
blind but channelling earth and
everything between the fragrant molecules
and always finding room for the air.
The worm is what we are heirs of
and there is no harm, much good,
in our being from there.

II.

I did so many things right;
I know that, but not always.
Now it is hard to look in the bathroom mirror.
So often I held you up after your bath,
wrapped in a towel, your head wet, eyes shining;
I held you up, heavy,
as though you were still a baby
and couldn't walk, to see your other self,
your name reversed, the boy in the mirror
and his mother, as happy as we.
He doesn't come now
to look at me from his side,
laughing and damp.
It is hard to look in
where he was, and won't be.
Where you were.

     ❂   ❂   ❂

I am so glad to sleep late in the morning
and not awake for a while to your absence.
Your nearby room is still so full of you.
It hurts to go in and find your things

waiting so quietly, nothing moved
and not even the faintest breath.
This is what's left of life
after your death, nothing
I can put together to make you.

✿   ✿   ✿

Your soul departed in a silent thunderclap.
Your body fell to the floor, and already
I knew no one could do anything more
for you, though everyone tried after that.
There was no going back.
It was terrible to know.

It is terrible to know now
as I look at all these little things
all I have left.

✿   ✿   ✿

They revived what they could of you
but then they gave up and they
counselled us to give up too.
It was not hard to do
after seeing your body burning

and seizuring on its own,
no one home, no lights on anywhere,
your eyes not opening.
We agreed to take the tubes out
and the nurse helped lift you
for the last time into your father's lap
so he could rock the last of you
in the white chair.
Surely, you died again, quietly,
in a few minutes. I helped wash
your hair and your young skin,
honoring with the water what was left
and not feeling such pain because

you had given me such a look before
you fell down dead the first time.
Your living eyes said we loved
and that you were going
and there was no coming back.
You console me with that look,
which is why you staggered
toward me, not toward death.

☼   ☼   ☼

Now I can see that
this is what we make of things.
The linear, the literal are tools
to help a gardener, but don't describe
the foxglove's vibrant mystery.
When I recount your death —
and oh, I do — I don't get anywhere.
You tried to tell me that.
You died, but dead isn't you.

❂   ❂   ❂

Now I can see that everywhere
is what a church should be.
The kitchen floor, where you fell,
is a homely altar; there
I burned the candles.
I moved your shrine then
to the white surface of the stove
and watched the last flame dance
to the music of the dervishes
your father played to help us.
How that flame danced, as you danced,
and went out, as you did,
when always I thought
you would go on, dancing.

❁ ❁ ❁

The raspberries are running
into your garden, trying to take over
the whole place! I have found it hard
to pull up any living thing.
Your hollyhock is the grandest plant,
planning its stately staff of flowers
as though you would be there to see it!
There is no real reasoning with the garden.
There is no mentioning your death
or asking the flowers the reason.
Anyway, they know all about you.
They are always taking you
into their considerations.
Among them, I have repaired
my circle of seashells
despite the failure of all my spells
to keep you safe from harm.
Did I ask the wrong thing,
or the wrong way?
Is there any use to asking?
Or is there only basking under the sun
and gathering up enough rain
to make a summer, and seeing that

pleasure and pain bind every molecule,
bind each soul, even when the sun goes in.
Still, I ask my lily sisters
for whatever they can give.
Now you are dead, I watch them
to learn to live.

❁   ❁   ❁

So many things to tell you!
Can I assume you know,
you hear me murmuring news
aloud in the garden?
How well this grows, and that?
How something comes up where
we didn't plan it, and this
we thought was lost!
The news of the garden is far from bad,
though slugs like beads on an abacus
trouble our calculations.
I wish you were here to see
some of what I see,
and whatever wonderful thing
you would find on your own.

❁   ❁   ❁

Now I can only walk beside the lake,
not follow the cold white path of mourning
onto it. The seagulls make such sad noises.
The waves come in, and I can trust them.
Everyday is almost the same. Sometimes
a loon, or a pair of mergansers, or
yesterday's mother and dozen baby ducks.
I find beautiful rocks; some are keepsakes.
But I can walk and walk, and never get
past time or into understanding.
Peace passes it, yes, I see that.
But I can only take so much of it.

❁   ❁   ❁

You said you didn't want to grow up
and have a moustache! What looked so bad
about that? Even I have a little one here,
a memory of our androgyny. What got you
so worried about growing up? A moustache,
the need to choose a wife, a few things
like that worried you right out of life?

❁   ❁   ❁

Now I am eating apricots
I bought for you, when you

loved their sweetness and
the orange plunge of
your young teeth into them.
They have outlasted you.
I eat them like prayers,
as though you are eating them.

❂   ❂   ❂

My grief comes first, but all around
are those who grieve for you,
who have your wound.
Our parents grieve for you,
and all their tears are sacraments.
And all our friends, of every age,
cannot believe that you are gone
and they are forced to grieve.
Your father, absent at your fall,
expects like me to hear your voice,
your call. We can't believe
that you are gone, at all.

❂   ❂   ❂

The squirrel has been hanging from
the bird feeder by her back feet,

shucking the seeds while upside-down
and showing me her rows of sore nipples.
So many mouths to feed.
So I throw some handfuls of seed
down on the ground for her,
to make life easier.
To feed you, though you aren't here,
and to feed me.

❂   ❂   ❂

Legacies came in the mail today:
the letter thanking us for the use
of your parts, your heart's valves
(others, we already know, are seeing
with your small corneas);
a copy of his will, naming me
among the many beloved
he leaves some money to;
my ticket to see our family
who will be grieving with me
that this time
only I am arriving.

❂   ❂   ❂

It is raining this afternoon.
This morning I brought home the tall weeds —
Bouncing Betty, Dame's Rocket,
pale purple flowers nodding on long stems —
and tamped them into the fresh ground
of our garden. Wilting immediately,
they bowed themselves and drooped
their leaves. Now I am hoping
the rain will revive them; indeed
I will go out in the rain to see,
thinking of you and your scattered molecules,
taken apart — and what can
that mean? I will tell
the Bouncing Bettys how you bounced too.

          ❂   ❂   ❂

Well they are not very happy
about it yet, their translation;
they were happy enough
where they were, rocketing by
the railroad tracks some blocks away.
It's their roots I am so aware of,
how to comfort them here,
if not with the rain.

Maybe if I still had some ashes of you
to spread around them they
would understand why I brought them
and be content. But I have let
what's left of you go over the sea
for burial by one of your grandfathers,
also newly dead. There your molecules
will do whatever they now do best.

❁   ❁   ❁

I am drinking water all day,
like a plant. The surest thing to do!
We should be wet inside; we are,
and that's why when your body burned
there was just a little box of ashes left.
We hardly knew what to do with it.
It sat on your bed, wrapped in your jacket,
and the cat slept beside it night after night,
now that your door was always open.

❁   ❁   ❁

Open and closed — the words at the center.
Nobody really knows what happens next.
I think of your feet, your toes in always

discolored socks, and how I reached
behind my car seat as we drove anywhere
to feel your firm consistency, your squirming
both with joy at my caress, and to insure
your separateness. I'd hold your feet;
you were behind me, I couldn't see you,
you were there always, and now
what can I make of the air?

✪   ✪   ✪

Pagans burn the bodies of their dead;
I read that somewhere. I confess
there was no other choice in my distress;
you were not cut roses going into a box
for delivery elsewhere. Surely your little smoke
was seen by stars, by birds,
by travelling grasshoppers, by grains
that drift beyond the limitations
of this world of ours. Surely
you left me with these openings.

✪   ✪   ✪

Oh, we knew that summer day
you were bound to let the balloon go —

hardly any child resists! Who could,
given the alternative! But I never expected
how you'd mourn for it, turning
at moments of sadness to its talisman,
saying "I miss my green balloon!,"
temporarily inconsolable. That small bright thing
stayed with you through three seasons,
a reappearing grief. So I take a leaf
out of your book when I miss you so.

        ✿   ✿   ✿

"I can wade grief, whole pools of it"
Mrs. Wells said, in our Latin class.
I can see her red head and her heavy glasses
and how she walked, stalked the hard linoleum
muttering poetry to minors, evoking
a great mythology. How she walks
in my head, now that I need the strength
that line seemed to give her, whenever
she said it, long ago, far away —
Ruth, Ruth Wells — Are you among the living?

        ✿   ✿   ✿

I would run up to her like an ancient mariner
holding your little picture in my hand
and asking her, How do I wade this loss?
Out of the ocean I came, out of the wet salt,
and here I am finding it wear upon my face.
How do I wade, Ruth, my own tears?
How do I hold back
such an amphibian?

       ✪   ✪   ✪

The phone rang, and I didn't answer it.
I will say I was outside looking at
the Bouncing Bettys, but really I was crying
and thinking of you, and working on
this long lament.

       ✪   ✪   ✪

I sent my taxes in recently.
I see they kindly include a notice
for those who find this
ridiculously difficult:
"Before you contact us,"
with some messages about documents.
I am astray among the documents,

wills, and certificates —
here they affirm your birth
and here your death. And his,
the man who left me something.
Who left you stories of travelling
up and down the continents by sea,
he was a sailor, nothing stopping him until
his heart popped on the white table.
You made fables of what he gave you:
my Uncle Johnny became your Brother Bill,
driving big trucks from one pole to the other
and sailing along the coast of Norway
just as he did, on the Murmansk run.
Your last picture shows a smiling face
on a great ship, and the shivering
flanks of Norway indubitably drawn.

❁   ❁   ❁

Now a man has come to the door
with a bouquet of Star-gazer lilies,
my favourite kind. Who could resist
this essential pink, these brown specks?
And the lilies opening like the first thing
on their long necks. If everything

is about coincidence how do I
respond? Am I unrolling like
the fronds of ferns or finding a flower?
You flowered from us and you died,
like Murray's lilies broken in a storm,
brought here to raise their heads like these
while you looked on, charmed.
I can interpret as I please
but oh, I am still alone, I am
so alone, and you don't come to me
even in my dreams!

       ✿   ✿   ✿

The lilies are from poets, now that I
read the card. It is not so unexpected.
They would find me wading my griefs
and thinking hard, musing, on all
the mysteries. There is such beauty
and it cannot last! We cannot ask it to!
All these stately lilies pass, and me, and you,
and as the poets say, the roses.
Somehow I hold on to
how lovely whatever it was
when it was here, the figured
molecules. The Star-gazer lilies. You.

There Has to Be

Death, so unimaginable,
came into our house and took you,
small one, and I saw you fall.
I saw your soul depart,
your body done for.
I saw the white stiff shell of you
wrapped and ready for burning.
So far as I know, you are gone.

But even so, it is not possible.
Even so, it is wrong.
I have made no further arrangements
in my mind. We leave your bed made,
all your things in place, knowing
there has to be some mistake.

And every morning I awake
thinking this is the day
when this impossible plasticity
will give itself a shake,
remake our true togetherness.

The sun comes up, so why not you,
out of your sleep, my small one?

I weep to find it isn't so,
and wait, again, hoping this
forsakenness is not to be my lot.
Today, life forgot what it should do,
forgot you for another day.
But it cannot continue.
You being you, us being us,
so much more than
ash, earth, and dust.

After Auden's "September 1, 1939"

Was it Eros then
who animated your dust,
your very mortal clay?
Was it Eros's grace
I saw pass away
from your much-loved face
when you fell that day?

It was not your body I loved
alone, though I loved it dearly
while you were in it, but in that
moment or dreadful minute
after your fall I knew the worst
would be to be left with only this,
if breath were there but not spirit.

Spirit of air, of Eros,
you departed, leaving me here,
my heart enlarged and then deserted.
Love still dwells; a light shines
where I work. Often I use it
to illuminate your portrait,
and to heal my hurt.

Letter to Auden

Ah, you miss in a diligent,
even a sad way, but not as I miss
someone, who have sat on Mary's throne!
Who have loved my own small golden one
and seen him cast down by death
from the shelter of my arms.
You men have been no pietà,
holding the lifeless body of the love you bore
before you, as though asking another celestial favor.
With your halo hollow, and pricking
the beating blood of you with its pointed stars!

Impressions

When we came home from the hospital
after you died, your father went out
and took photographs of your bootprints
left in the snow, not that the shapes told much,
sunk in the winter white, mere negatives
of the pressure of your life!
It is hard to explain to those who were not here
what makes these odd, last photographs so dear.

Yet I refused the nurse's offer
to ink the palms of your dead hands
and the soles of your dead feet
and press them to a piece of paper.
Would the ink have been left on you then,
like marks of consecration?
And I refused to cut a lock of your hair.
I have your keepsakes here in the heart,
here and thus everywhere!

But I have been tempted to bring home
some sand from the beach where a year ago
you played, as though some grain you touched
might have stayed your magic. As though
I could find one, identify it as such!
But oysters make much out of so little.
Should I keep your DNA in a locket?

Connecting

The psychic says when you died I died too —
at least that part of me died
and crossed over to the other side with you
and I must retrieve that part
as though it were on a tether.
But I was wondering whether it might not work
like the experimental telephone you made in school,
two paper cups connected by a string that is knotted
at their centers. The string can be very long,
as long as it's tight. My own, let's try to get
this current experiment right. It matters.
You are the one who asked me, unexpectedly,
"Do you lose your voice when you die?"
Now I would like to give a different answer.

Remnants

What're we to do with your broken dumptrucks
that you loved so much, and all the rusting toys
in the sandbox? They are divested
of their always precarious worth, these wrecks
that once were the best-loved dumptrucks on earth.

I will keep your bear, who lived in a box.
You made Christmas lights for him last year,
colored blots on carefully cut garlands of paper.

In Santa's sleigh made out of blocks
on the living-room carpet you flew
on your way, calling your greetings and waving,
holiday music playing on a tape.

And you drew a two-headed angel,
you drew things happening at the Pole
in teetering igloos with flags
festooning them like those of explorers.
Smiling faces peer from many of the icy rooms.

You drew over and over the Tree of winter
splendid with lights and birds.

Letters and words stagger across your pages
learning their legibility — but now
they make no progress.

Toys, art, you dead —

my own part is considering whether or not
there is an extra head on this odd angel.

Considering

It is easy to think that things in life are random
until the most unlooked-for comes to you.
Then there must be a pattern,
or you abandon your bit of safety.
I feel a big X like a target on top of my head
that marked me as a mother whose child
would become dead.
I feel I should wear a cardboard sign that says
PITY AND FEAR ME BOTH: MY CHILD HAS DIED.
I know there is much suffering in this wide world,
and that often it seems like an accident.
But now that the people involved are you and I
it is impossible to believe.
My lament revolves around the yearning for answers.
Thus — did you come to us or were you sent?
Then — did you leave by choice or were you taken?
I think your life describes a certain course,
but I may be mistaken.

Some Communications

Debbie had said to us months before
that you were an old soul — old at four!
Sandra and Dennis had noticed when you were a baby
that you were remarkably aware of mood —
maybe you knew a lot already.
Maybe our understanding is too crude.
Norah the psychic asked me if you'd said
anything to indicate you knew you would be dead
and yes, you had. You had said you would miss me.
(You added, you would miss me when *I* died.
But *I* didn't.)

And you told stories of another town
where you knew everyone for miles around,
and all the animals, horses and dogs,
named Cut-down and Tanglewood and things like that,
and Dark, the cat, who won a cat race.
You told these stories with such
certainty on your face, as more than
a wild or wistful imagining.

You had brothers and sisters and cousins there,
and other parents. How I'd like to hear
from your other mother now, if you are with her,
telling her stories about us!
How can I ask her to send word,
perhaps only your name on some kind of postcard,
those well-known, love-smoothed syllables!
As I wish I had sent some word to her
when you were here — to let her know
I was willing to share —

I Have Learned More Quietly in the Garden

From the hummingbirds.
They come suddenly, out of
the other side of life,
with wings like I
could never have.
They just appear,
quietly as nothing,
beautifully there.
One came a moment ago
to the flowers
of my son's oregano.
My son who is dead.
One came to take a shower
while I was watering the garden
with the hose. I stood so still then!
One came speeding down the air
and when it saw me
turned so sharply
I was startled.
Away it went!
Such small beings!
How they come and go.
How they are the garden.

For the Pelican

Pelican, white pelican,
you took a slow, lazy swoop
over our backyard wedding —
to see what was going on?
Or were you bringing the soul
of our boy, to join
the string of molecules in me?
Had he been riding your feathery back
downriver, to drop off and drift in
and be part of everything from the start?
To add to the string of pearls
his beating heart?

White pelican, it is six years later
and you may still be fishing somewhere,
basking away the winter in the south,
but our boy died. His aunt dreamed
he was diving into water, smiling,
bringing silvery fish out.
So, is he with you?

Sometimes I imagine he is wearing
the white dress of whirling dervishes,
learning their dance,
the trance that connects them
to earth and sky.

Or I imagine a pelican
flying by —

For the Sky

Right after you died, I woke up
with the silence in your room at night,
no sleepy scuffling or breathing noises.
All too quiet! Then I began to sleep
so deeply. My third ear, my third eye
disappeared, leaving no visible scars.
Or I could say that my ocean of caring for you
dried up, leaving quiet sand, quiet stars.

So I am standing
at the edge of the desolation
that used to be filled with you.
I stare up at the sky,
as though you have evaporated.
This is why we look for angels,
why we listen in shells for the sea.

For the Earth

You knew me truly
from the inside out
like no one else
like I knew you

And yet, you knew me best
as SHE, Beginning and End,
the All, the We,
WITHOUT WHICH NOT

Thus when you woke
you came to me, the rock,
to get your strength
and when you hurt, the same

when you needed a nap
I had the safe and sacred lap
no other

I often resisted
being a Goddess
Mother my only name

I struggled to be myself
despite your crown
and yet, my boy,
I knew it for my own

I try to wear it now
when you are gone

And Yet, No Crown —

The apes embrace their own
like I —

the lioness bereft
does mourn —

the grief at heart's the same —

Otherwise I am thinking of elevated Mary
wearing a halo for the moon
eclipsed by it, her mother's love
a rune, a tomb

Did she mourn a God or a son?
And when? And how?
There's room for confusion
as I know now.

Mary and Her Boy

What would she say about why she loved him?
When, from the beginning, he was hardly hers.
In all the portraits she barely holds him.
He clearly doesn't need her mothering.

So would she say she loved him as his Father's son?
For sermons? For being wise before he was born?
For having to die for a great purpose?
Or that he danced on sunlight on the floor,
greeted the Christmas lights on trembling tiptoe,
was kind to other little children,
had wonderful conversations with her,
warm in her warm arms.

One of Many

This photograph is haunting
because in it you are lying still, asleep,
surrounded by pillows and blankets and toys.
You woke up sometime after this
to eight more months of life.
And then I saw you dead, the last breath
coming out of you, and then
partly revived on the hospital tables
but when the nurse opened your eye mechanically
and shone a light on it there was no response.
Your muscles relaxed differently
than when you were most alive.
And then I saw you dead for the last time
and wrapped in your white Muslim winding cloth
in your white box of a coffin.
You looked like you do in this picture
and yet not like.
Here, where you lie asleep
I want to go back in time
and hold you again and have you warm,
waking up into the rest of your life.
I want every moment back
when I did hold you.

Your Sorrow

I walk around with my invisible black armband, my reflecting shield of grief, feeling vulnerable behind it to the stares of passing strangers and only able to find some relief in the enclosure of my home and wandering like a lost explorer over the white pages that I chase with ink. But sometimes when I am out I am aware of all the sorrows in the air, what you might carry and you and you, each of us privileged by our individual tragedies and no one able to assign a scale or make prophetic sense of the great weight of disbelief. We trudge, we smile, we make conversation and discuss occurrences, only sometimes sharing what is first in our minds, what we relive in memory and reconstruct in the imagination. Then we are able to show our candles sheltered by the frail shield of our hands.

But I can do no more now than acknowledge your possible sorrow as we pass in the street; I am rubbed too raw by grief to speak.

The Mourners

The Mourners came to our house in little flocks with shocked, still faces and hands bearing gifts of food and messages and candles and flowers. We became a shrine and the things piled up on all the tables, vases stately with tall carnations and roses and the sad fronds of ferns, the refrigerator filled with the usual responses to sorrow: casseroles and brownies, soup and biscuits. Mourners sat in all the chairs and stood in the kitchen and looked for the ready box of tissues. Written words piled up too, so few of them truly satisfying.

Soon I began to see that some of the mourners came out of their own sadnesses, so well reminded of what happened to them another time another place, of who sickened or turned away and who died. I heard the stories. I saw in others the wish to appease the gods and keep grief off them by acknowledging ours.

I let everyone in, spoke on the phone, turned our home into the gate of mystery, tried to insist that though death had a hand in this joy was paramount, that I knew even

as I suffered in every bit of marrow every stretch of
sinew that you, my little one, still lived, live, in some
way that we scarcely know.

So I am thrown back on the shores of the old religions
where as a girl I had been wont to go, thinking because
I was young I understood. But there are no general rules
in such cases, no places where the whispering grove
whispers the same words over and over for all to hear.
The mourners must come from wherever they are with
whatever they know and lay down their carefully cho-
sen gifts, and lift their faces to the light in the sky which
is the first light we see by and the one we hold in our
hearts, in the small shrine we build there to the beauty of
life and love and the knowledge that on occasion neither
is enough. Through the small trees in the shrine of my
heart comes the small occasional wind, murmuring that
you live in joy, as you always did. This wind is kind and
I listen to it when it comes, yes, sometimes telling the
other mourners what it says.

Death Has Your Face

I have seen death only a few times — with the old cats, as I held them, getting a shot and suddenly loose in their muscles, tongues sticking out a bit, easy and painless. Now you, seizing and falling, filled to the top of your lungs with fluids caused by the viruses. But no pain showed, only the faintest surprise. You looked at me as you died, affirming our relationship. Then you fell and made your death rattle.

How could I be afraid of death now, having seen you die? Seeing your death come over your beloved features? Death on this occasion looked like you, not some shadowy grim reaper. I know this is unusual, but is it not a gift, to see at one end of the mysterious spectrum? Death has your face and thus a sacred place in me.

✿   ✿   ✿

And *sacred place* — you died in our house, in our very kitchen, in the heart of all our care. Despite all I could do for you, death came in and found you there. Looking like you and in the center of my love. How do I read this riddle? Noah's dove came back empty-beaked, as though they floated on nothing at all; Noah believed but also the dove lived to make another try.

Whereas I am high and dry on my Mount Ararat needing something feathery or fluid to find me. I have no messengers to send. There is nothing inspiring about the view. It feels like an end that cancels further beginnings. The bleakness of life without you.

The Worst Loss

People tell me this is the worst loss, what happened to us, to you, your easy death at home, even though you hardly knew you were sick, invaded by viruses and pushed in a rush over the brink of life. You had time to give me a last look before you left. The worst loss — because you were small and still innocent according to all the religions; the worst loss even for those who believe you have gone directly to heaven and are even now an angel at the feet of God.

But I say NO, NO, it is not the worst, not the worst way to die and with no human hand raised against you, not stolen, molested, maimed or burned, blown apart, murdered or decapitated. Of all the possible deaths you had one of the best, one most of us hope for ourselves when we consider it.

That you were young and able and full of potential, yes I admit there is a great grief to your cancellation, to the end of my pride in you, my delight in your doings, even your terrible tantrums aligned to vitality. But oh my dear, I am unable to say that you did not accept your death, that it is not for the best, that otherwise your life would have been as perfect as the perfect glory of a highbred hothouse flower, that you would have lived till 90 unscathed doing great deeds, adding to our human depth, rich in your personal gifts and enjoying every minute. I cannot say anything like that, had no guarantees and could offer none to you, gave you birth and couldn't save you from this one rare eventuality.

I know nothing well enough anyway, knew you and didn't, saw there were things in you larger and more hidden and more beautifully mysterious than anything my mind could devise. I would look into your eyes and not be able to read you, though we knew each other truly.

Life is full of things and occurrences I do not understand, and that is just as it should be, I am not big enough to encompass all possible knowledge and impossible sense.

But I am not saying any God had anything to do with this, punishing us or you or providing an example to drive the flock inside the fence. I cannot accept any outside agent but the cunning viruses and more than that your own love and intelligence with their mysterious depths.

Just as I only partially understood you (and not that I understand myself) I only partially comprehend your death, wondering who recently left this little beautiful piece of weathered glass on the shore and who blew out the ceremonial candle when I asked, if not you?

By This Little Water

This is not at all like the sea
this little rill of melt water
yet it surely comforts me
a self-acknowledged
water daughter
as it chatters
of little matters
effortlessly
soothing my grief
itself unheeding

I am not a daughter of snow, oh no,
though I crunch it under my boot soles
it is too quiet and too cold
smoothing grief into sleeping

So at the end of winter
drifted in snow
by this little water
I sit listening

Alone

We wind up the year,
headed for the anniversary
of your death, that cold day.
Your father and I play solitaire
separately, so often alone
in our grief, our minds elsewhere
while our hearts stagger.
What matters? What?
Or who? For we who know
that the essential magic
can remove itself in a sleight of hand,
the simple questions lose their answers.
The Jacks are ready to wink;
the Queens and Kings are flat as paper.
The year slowly tapers
to the memory of our sad event:
the day when you left
and our joy was spent
all in a moment.

When You Died

What do I go by?
The moon, the calendar date,
the day of the week it was?
None of it makes sense,
so out of the normal reckoning.
There is no single anniversary of your death,
no formal moment beckoning
for marking what has gone
and what is left.
We drank a feeble toast to you,
I light an ordinary candle.

Little

I thought it was you
making ponds in the soapdish
with your little hands after washing.
I thought it was you
spraying the toilet with pee
that made it stink.
But now you are no excuse,
and when I clean the same bathroom
I see your efforts
to climb up into the sink
because it was there
and you were little
and had ambition.

Lost

Lost — you are a *loss*,
but did I *lose* you?
Are you findable?
Really, I'd refuse to talk to you
on some celestial telephone
except to say "Come home!"
in an angry and desperate voice.
I'd hang up before you explained
that your going wasn't by choice
or that it was — I don't care
what you're up to in your other dimension!
Let me in there and I'll make a fuss!
Register nearly universal dissension!
Everything and everyone on Earth agrees
you belong right HERE, with us.

Another Photograph

You look like you are
singing in this tree,
like you popped out of a burl
instead of me
and belong to a different world
where you steady yourself
on the bole of thoroughly living

You look like you could
sing for everything
like you are the epitome
of tree/air/boy/being
as though there are no distinctions
in such whole joy

(and no leaving, no grieving)

So present are you
even now
in this flat thing

Praise

When Owen danced on sunlight
all was praise, and so
it should be.
His small, bare boy feet thumped
among the shining rays
to a spry boy beat
now dark, now bright,
shadows leaping beneath
a boy in warm gold giggling,
prancing, light arrayed,
splendid!
So he made
the sun's ordinary entrance
into an invitation
all those dancing days,
all those dancing days.

The Day When Owen Saw the Dolphins

Slap the water
and these dolphins come
thinking you have a gift
of fish

for them
at the edge of
the ocean

full of fish
but they like
gifts

    ✿   ✿   ✿

you, first, saw their
partial shapes
their fins

little, you
recognized them
you knew their name

you stood there with me
as I slapped the surface

in they came

racing our heartbeats
making us long to swim
while reverencing the distance
between us and them

the difference:
changing line of shore
riffle of water

I had no gifts
of fish
for them

they swam
like melodies
through music
moving
off

✿   ✿   ✿

Now you
have shape-shifted
swim
in the ill-defined
ocean
after death

I stand
at various edges
calling you
slapping this page

wondering if I'll
recognize you
understand
the music

Do I have
what it takes?

the gifts

the
¿¿fish??

In Owen's Garden

In Owen's garden, in early spring, the flowers were the first up, way out in the yard where it shouldn't be warm enough yet. A swirl of brown earth among the receding skirts of snow, and blooming crocuses that had the year before been potted flowers brought by friends for the funeral. I planted out all the funeral flowers that came in pots and they all lived over the winter, Owen, the first winter you've been gone, and your little garden was the earliest flowering place in the whole town. Crocuses followed by bright hyacinths and tulips, there where two years before you had planted carrots and cucumbers. And the chrysanthemum, the hydrangea, and the rosebush, meant to comfort us once, have also lived, put on green again, and are growing robust.

Your hollyhock, dear son, had six tall stalks last year, the tallest at seven feet or more, as though it were going somewhere by growing UP. Such megaphones of flowers — with something to say, for more than bees. This year the leaves are huge, and I am interested to see how many and how tall the stalks will be, and whether or not by listening intently to the flowers I will be able to gather anything new. Anything more about you.

A friend told me today a recent dream in which you came and sat on her lap and hugged her and said you loved her, more demonstrative than you normally were. In the dream, she needed comfort from someone, and you were the one who came. I am not a good rememberer of my own dreams, though I know you appear in them. But in waking life there are the many loving coincidences that reverberate, that germinate into messages, into tall-growing certainties.

I learn a lot from your garden, from this exuberant hollyhock, so much like your beautiful self. It reminds me that though you are gone, dear Owen, in the garden of our love it is springtime.